Forex for Beginners: Making Money With

A Step by Step Guide to Currency Trading: How to be a Successful Part-Time Forex Trader

Table of Contents

Introduction 1

Chapter 1: What is Forex? 3

Chapter 2: Why Trade in Currencies? 13

Chapter 3: How to Become a Success 29

Chapter 4: How to Make this a Part Time Job 57

Chapter 5: Attitude for Winning 61

Chapter 6: Recap 65

Conclusion 67

Introduction

Thank you for choosing this book as your guide to stepping out into the world of Forex. In this book, you will learn all the basic information you need to start understanding foreign exchange currencies, and how to trade them. You will learn exactly what Forex is, and why you should dabble in the art of trading it. You will learn about the risk vs. the reward, and much much more. All lined out with clear and concise instructions, tips, and other indicators to make this book simple and enjoyable to read. I hope you find what you need, and that this book is what gives you the push to start this fun adventure in the currency trading world.

Chapter 1: What is Forex?

Forex is the trading of currencies across a foreign market. Forex is literally short for foreign exchange. This asset class exchanges one country's currency for another, which allows people to use it for a variety of things, but the most common is tourism. Forex sets a standard rate for exchanging currencies, and this allows people to be protected from fluctuation risks. Seeing as this is a global industry, you have to deal with countries in their native currency. Back before the influx of the internet, currencies were allowed to just float around and fluctuate at will, until investors and banks took interest in it, and set a standard rate of exchange in which to back the currencies off of.

Foreign Exchange Market

This is a market that has to do with everything in the foreign exchange market. You can buy, speculate, sell, or even exchange currencies. This market is made up of banks and companies, brokers and investors, and much much more.

These firms and people make it possible to have a steady exchange rate in foreign currencies, to reduce risk of fluctuation.

Forex provides a floor for speculation and processing of currencies, along with conversion and investment of currencies. It has a high rate of success, and draws in many people from across the board.

There are many reasons why this market is desirable.

- Flexible Hours: This market is open for 24 hours Monday through Friday. It is only closed on the weekends. This means that someone who works a normal nine to five job, or someone enrolled in school, can still access the benefits of currency trading on their time off, without having to interrupt their daily routine.

- Large Industry: Forex is the largest industry in the world of finance, with several banks, and outlets to choose from, there is always a space for a new investor or trader in the market. With over four trillion dollars traded daily, billions of that was in currency and options trading.

- High Assets: Being one of the most impressive assets in the world, Forex has some high liquidity. That means that any assets you put into this process will be safer than anywhere else. There will always be money to be made in this industry

- High Leverage: The amount of leverage in this business is astounding. You can have a thousand dollars and trade it for a hundred thousand dollars worth of currency. This is the best part of Forex trading. It gives you the power to become powerful. You will earn money without having to work extremely hard. You just have to learn a few things and let the leverage work itself out

With perks like that, it is impossible not to be intrigued by this amazing investment opportunity. The ability to make money so easily is worth every penny you put into it. Forex trading is simple, as long as you are willing to put in a little money, and learn about exchange rates.

Being the biggest currency industry out there, there are always openings, so you don't have to worry about fighting for a spot. All you have to be willing to do is try to get in. A little bit of knowledge, and a whole lot of confidence, and you will you be on your way.

Breaking down the market is pretty simple as well. It is not centrally located, but is a global market that has so many different outlets it will make your head spin. The exchange rates are also not set with profit in mind, but standards and policies, which means they can't be changed at whim. This is a good thing, because going in, you will know the basic exchange rate, and will be informed well in advance of any changes. This is unlike any other investment market where things can change in the blink of an eye.

A Forex broker may act as a market maker in his area as well, if there are no major banks in play. It would be up to him (or her) to set the rate, and it would be in a personal best interest to set the exchange rates at a competitive rate to ensure that he or she has a lot of business in the near future, because most people prefer to deal with banks rather than straight brokers, as banks have stricter policies. However, human nature to get the best deal often wins out, bringing a broker who has chosen to be competitive more business, therefore ensuring the broker a profit.

The market also relies on a network of computers to run properly. These networks keep documentation of exchange rates around the world, and a person interested can look up and see where you would go to get the best exchange rate, or if there is any fluctuation in exchange rates. These computer networks are what made Forex possible, because before the internet came around, exchange rates were very volatile. They would change from one hour to the next.

That is why Forex is such a good industry today. All the people in the network are working hard to keep the exchange rates fairly normal, and never go back to the dark times of foreign exchange again.

History of Forex

Currency exchange goes way back into biblical times. As long as currency has existed, it has needed to be exchanged for one reason or another. This is because the world has never once agreed upon a currency as a standard. The reason for this is that money was made out of what was most common for the area. For example, in China, gold was the most common. However, in areas like Saudi Arabia, in ancient times, their crops and livestock were their currency. However, when you went to the Temple once a year, (people traveled hundreds of miles on foot to go to the Temple) the tithe had to be of one currency. Either silver or gold, whatever was more available that year. This meant that they had to have someone to exchange their currencies. The people who exchanged these currencies were referred to Kollybistes, and they set up during Feast Time at the Temple once a year. These people were ruthless, they often charged high exchange fees, and looked down upon the poor, often charging them higher fees than the rich. These men were not in it to help people find spirituality, but rather to help line their own pockets for the year. These people did not care about actually exchanging money, and often jacked the exchange rate up at whim, so they could have a larger profit, often stealing from the church, because that lowered the amount of money that people could give.

You have to realize that unlike now, there was no way that most of these people could have access to more currency than what they brought with them. They often brought a few small animals, or a small bag of local coins, or a small amount of crops, whatever their tithe may have been, and walked with these for hundreds of miles. They often started their journey two to three months in advance to get to the Temple in time. They spent half a year traveling, and if they were lucky, they made it their alive without being accosted by robbers. So these people arrived with not much more than the clothes on their backs, and a few chickens or what have you, only to be told that they do not have enough currency to make a proper tithe, so they have to settle for less, and repent for their sins and hope that their measly tithe would cover all the sins they committed that year.

If you are familiar with the Christian Bible, you probably know the story of when Jesus flipped the table. (If you are not of Christian religion, I do apologize, merely making a reference.) Well in the story, or parable if you will, Jesus came across the Temple during feast times. He saw these horrible Kollybistes taking advantage of people for their own profit, and was furious. He felt that any tithe available should be good enough for his Father, as people gave him the best they had. The Kollybistes were taking advantage of people's fear of Hell, and using it to line their pockets and fill their bellies. He was so angry that he flipped these large tables over in the courtyard, and screamed at these scam artists.

This was not the only time that currency trading was monopolized, however. The Byzantine empire, in the fourth century, monopolized the trade of foreign currencies as well. The Emperor wanted to make as much profit as he possibly could off of foreign currency exchanges, as he wanted visitors to literally pay to visit his empire. This created a major problem toward the end of this reign though, as many people decided to quit visiting the Byzantine empire. They wanted nothing to do with the monopolizing of tourism, or currency exchange. The Emperor relied so much on visitors as an income source, that the empire fell, and could not be rebuilt.

All throughout time, currency exchange has been essential to people buying and selling goods, such as pottery, cloth, even food. The exchange rates in that time fluctuated so much that you never knew if you were getting a good deal or if you should wait an hour to see then. Currencies were not standardized until early modern times.

In the early eighteen hundreds, a well know Italian family by the last name of Medici decided that there needed to be a safer way to hold your money. They established the worlds first bank, and all foreign exchange of currencies in the area had to be done there. Along with deciding that there had to be a controlled environment for exchanging currencies, the Medici family also decided that there should be a standard currency backing all trade. Gold was chosen as the standard monetary backer. This continued for several years, until the beginning of world war one. People left the gold standard propelled by the onset of war, in hopes of gaining more control of international trade.

After the war, the pound sterling was very popular in the foreign exchange business. Cheaper than the gold backing, it was also less reliable. By this time, many different countries had jumped onto the forex bandwagon. Even the newly forming United States of America was in on it. England was pretty skeptical of the whole ordeal, however. In the beginning they only had two exchange brokers. However, they too began to see the benefits of forex, and by 1922,

Britain had jumped to seventeen bank backed brokers and over forty firms with forex brokers.

After world world two, the strict exchange rate of currency was ended, and currency exchanges were allowed to fluctuate again. This caused the market to crash, and even caused it to close for about a year. However, one good thing did come out of this. Computers became the latest technology, and replaced telephones for communication throughout the network.

After 1973, Forex was completely free floating, meaning there were no controls on where they could trade, however, every trade was gold backed. During this time, the United Nations had the highest rate of trade.

That is the history of Forex. It is necessary to know the history to make sure that you truly understand the entire process. Otherwise you will be out there floating blindly and not realizing what to look for. If you know what you are looking for, then you will be able to prevent any bad trades from ruining your bank account.

Chapter 2: Why Trade in Currencies?

Trading in currencies does have some risk, just like any other investment. Some people often lose money on a regular basis, and in some ways this market is more risky than others, however in other ways it is less risky. This market is extremely appealing to those who like to gamble as well, because it is considered a gamble.

Just like with any investment, currencies are a way to make money. You invest in an exchange, and make more money in that country than you have in your own. This allows you to have a little bit of control in your account, and you are able to hold that investment until you can exchange it with another country for a higher amount than you already have.

This seems like it is a little confusing, but it really is not. This is actually one of the simplest once you learn the basic rules of the business. That is what makes this industry so appealing, the ability to go into it without a degree in investing. It is simple to learn, and has a good success rate, as long as you don't get greedy.

This is a great industry for someone who wants to invest, but doesn't want to be super hands on. You can check in every so often, but you don't have to think about a whole bunch of different factors. You can leave the investing details to your broker.

As a plus, this market is very liquid. It is always increasing. At this point in the game, there is more than four billion dollars being transacted every single day. That means that there is over four trillion dollars available for profit every single day. This is a great thing for someone just getting into the market, as they have a great opportunity to achieve a good amount of profit. There are so many outlets and people involved in this market, that there is no shortage of people to seek advice from as well.

Forex has many opportunities to make it big.

You just have to have to know where to look, and how to operate your money in this business.

Here are some ways to have a great success:

- **Brokers**: Finding a good broker is always a good idea. A broker can make or break your account. You have to find a good one with a reputable reputation and good credentials. Make sure they are willing to discuss the process with you. Secretive ones could be scooping more out of your profit than you realize.

- **Research**: Even though this is a pretty easy market to navigate, that does not mean that you can go through it like a blind dog searching for a bone in a slaughter yard. You need to be well informed to know where you need to go in the industry to get the best outcome.

- **Fast paced environment:** This means that you can get in and get started quickly. The faster you can get started, the faster you can start making money. As an investor the best thing to do is start making money as quick as possible, because every month that you are not making money is technically a loss of money. You do not want to lose more money than you put into your investment, because that is how you go bankrupt. While this is not a get rich the minute you put money in business, it is a very fast paced environment, and can get you in a lot faster, allowing you to start making money faster than most investment jobs.

- **Good risk ratio**: This business is considered high risk by those who don't know the inner workings of the business, but in reality, if you know what you are doing, it has what is considered to be less risk than most investment industries. However the risk is more do or die than those industries. This makes for a good thrill in this industry and helps keep things interesting. The thrill of the industry makes it more captivating, which is good, because the more you focus on this business, the better you will succeed.

- **Less competitive:** This business is not very competitive at all. There are so many ways to make money that there is room for everyone in this game. You don't have to be a genius either, you just have to be willing to put in some time and eff0rt to make it. The best thing about not having any competition is that means more guaranteed money for you, and you don't have to worry about someone taking your spot in this game. This means you can focus even more on your investment without a care in the world as to who else is playing the game.

- **Margin based trading accounts**: This is kind of like grading on a scale. You have a little wiggle room with your investment, so if the scale slides a little, you won't go under. This can also be a little tricky, but it has some great benefits and offers great protection if you are a part of it. The ability to have a margin based account makes thing a lit easier on newbies who do not have a whole lot of investing experience.

- **Leverage:** This was brushed over briefly in the last chapter, but leverage is a great thing to have in investing, and if you have leverage you have a better chance of making it big in the business. The good thing about forex is that you have the potential to gain a lot of leverage. You can trade for larger positions than you ever thought would be possible for investments. Just because you don't have that in your account, does not mean that you can't make it. That is the great thing about this industry. You can make more money than you ever could imagine.

- **Profit:** The profit in this game is amazing. No matter what way the market is going you can still have the opportunity to make a profit. This is done by using short sales in forex, or selling a derivative before you buy it. This can make you a lot of money even if the market is going south. If the market is going good, you can make a great profit just by doing regular sales and exchanges. The possibilities are endless, and that is a wonderful thing.

There are many reasons why forex is a great opportunity for everyone. This industry is a great example of why you should definitely give investing a try. As an investor you have the opportunity to make a lot of money, and you get the thrill of a risk when you take one.

Forex is a business for everyone. You don't have to be a Wall Street executive to make it big in this company. In fact, here are a few success stories, and how each person achieved a good success in the business.

Success Stories

KIM A.

Kim was an elementary school teacher who wanted something a little more from her life. She wanted to take a risk, but not one with her life. She contemplated for years on what she could do to make her life more exciting, but could never come up with anything. That was until her friend told her about forex. She looked into it, and saw that it could be a very risky business, and that she could lose a lot of money. It was just the kind of risk she was looking for. One with the potential of a great reward. So she did her research and looked into every aspect of the business. Excitedly, she made an account, and started trading. Unfortunately, she got too greedy the first time. She lost over five thousand dollars in eight months. However, she did not let that discourage her. A few smarter investments later, and she was up and running again. She slowed her roll a little bit after realizing that the thrill meant serious money loss. She decided to make one risky investment instead of several.

This was four years ago, now she is still a teacher, but she only does it because she enjoys making an impact on kids' lives. She has a nice car, a new house, more money in her account than she ever knew was possible, and she continues to grow her investments. She has made it in this business, and she has some advice to all who want to try this out.

"Don't wait years to make the decision to jump. Decide today. The sooner you make the jump, the sooner you can screw up. Don't get discouraged if you make a bad investment. Learn from that mistake and try again. You have to have a few things go wrong to appreciate when things go right."

This is true of this industry. You have to try a few times before you can finally hit the jackpot. Kim learned this the hard way, and when she thought she had lost everything, she finally made it somewhere in the forex world.

JACK J.

Jack was a machine shop mechanic working forty plus hours a week when he decided he wanted something more. He waded through scheme after scheme that promised a get rich quick outcome. Knowing that everything real takes real work, he kept searching, thankfully not falling for the traps. He searched and searched every day, when one day he was at his local library, and he discovered a section on investing. He looked into several types of investments. He wanted something that he could do after a long work day, something that was flexible, and yet had good results. After some thorough searching, he came across forex. Forex literally changed his entire outlook on how you could make money. He thought you had to put in a lot of work to gain money. He was skeptical about it at first. He talked to a friend he knew in investing, and verified that this was a legit way to make money. Interested, he asked his friend to help him get started. He was excited, so he took a sizable portion of his savings, and handed it over to his friend. He was certain that he could trust his friend to handle the particulars. A few weeks later, he goes to see his friend, only to find that his friend has moved with no forwarding address, no number, nothing. Thankfully, he handed over cash, instead of banking particulars, so his friend only got away with the money he handed over.

Discouraged, Jack returned to his daily job, and put the thought of forex out of his mind. He worked hard to restore his savings to where they were at before he was ripped off by his friend. One day, Jack was looking through some articles online, and saw that the forex market was healthier than ever. It sparked his interest again, and this time he looked for a broker firm to help him out. He went with a highly recommended one, and after checking the credentials, and getting a definitive answer on how things worked, he took a small amount out of his savings to start out with. He handed it over, and kept in touch with the firm on how things were going. In about two months the two hundred dollars he had invested had grown to four hundred dollars. He decided to invest and trade a little more. His investments grew, and under a cautious hand, Jack took more control of his investments. He finally stepped away from a broker this year, after three years in the investment business. Now he is retired and living off his profit, as he enjoys his grand kids, and finally gets to spend plenty of time with his children.

He does have one piece of advice, however.

"Don't trust just anyone. You have to make sure that they do know what they are doing. And you have to be sure that they are backed with documents and signatures to ensure that they will not just run off with all of your hard earned money. Also, just because things go wrong once, does not mean they always will. Get back up on that horse, and try again."

This is great advice in this business. There are going to be people that want to tear you down, and who want to take advantage of your naivety, you have to be able to stay above them, and stay one step ahead of the poachers.

RAYMOND H.

Ray was a full time car salesman when he got into forex. He wasn't really looking for anything different, as he had a great job, with amazing benefits. He was just talking with a customer who had been a regular of their used car lot for years. One day this customer came in with the money to buy a brand new Lexus straight out, no loan or anything. So he was curious about how this everyday Joe could afford such a nice car all of a sudden. The customer told him about forex, and so Ray was intrigued. He decided to look into it. He dabbled a little bit in it, and for all intents and purposes made it a part time job. He became proficient at it, and even dabbled in some short sales when the market started to slip. He managed to make his impressive salary look meager. He was impressed that he was able to increase his earnings so exponentially with very little effort.

Ray didn't have many major pitfalls, as he had been in the loan business, and money business for many years working with the particulars of financing with cars, so he knew the ins and outs of dealing with tricky parts of money handling. He also knew that you needed a trusted money handler, so he did his due diligence. This made all the difference as he was able to make money faster, and lost very little. That isn't to say that he didn't lose money, he just didn't lose exponential amounts. He of course had a few slip ups. Everyone does. However his slips didn't really affect anything. Ray was one of the lucky ones, but of course he made sure to keep everything in order. And it is in that spirit that he offers this piece of advice

"Always do your research. No matter how excited you are, you have to take your time to make sure you cross your T's and dot your I's. You have to read about every aspect of this business, and then read again. It is deceptively simple. If you go in thinking you can blindly swing and hit a home run, then you need to rethink your approach, because I guarantee that you will miss. You have to make sure that you are prepared for everything that may happen. I cannot stress enough how easy it is to mess up, because you are under the impression that simple means easy to understand. You still have to learn a few things before you can consider yourself adept enough to take your investments into your own hands."

This is pertinent advice. The number one reason people fail in this market is that they don't do enough research. You have to read up very well on this subject, ask questions, and take it slow.

LISA C.

Lisa was a homemaker when she and her husband got divorced. Suddenly she found herself a single mom, with a newborn baby, and as she breastfed every two hours, she could not feasibly find a full time job. However she was getting a good alimony settlement from her ex husband. She decided that she would invest this money in forex, which she had heard of in her ex husband's business circle. She had been told that it was a great investment opportunity. She tool a portion that she did not absolutely need for home necessities, and her kids, and she invested that into a forex account. She made a bit of money that way, and excited for her success, she decided to make a really risky jump. This was a big mistake. She didn't have enough time to watch it and pull it when it began to crash, so she ended up losing all the money she had made and more.

This would have discouraged any normal person, but Lisa wanted to spite her ex so bad, that she tried again. She wanted to make enough money to be able to tear her ex's alimony check up in his face and watch it scatter in the wind. She hated living off of his money, knowing that he was with another woman. After a few more tries, Lisa found a great opportunity, and invested a good amount of money. The whole neighborhood could hear her scream of excitement when it paid off. This was the best feeling in the world for her. She had enough money to keep on with the investing while still living off her investment money for a few months. With a few more educated investments, she was able to live completely off of her investments, and she asked the courts to stop the alimony payments. She has this one piece of advice for anyone who wants to begin this tricky business.

"Don't get greedy. Don't let your emotions control you. You have to have a level head or else all of your investments will fall flat. Just because you want revenge, does not mean that you have to let it cloud your judgment."

Those are some great success stories that show you people from all walks of life succeeding at this business. Hopefully this convinces you that you too can succeed at forex.

Chapter 3: How to Become a Success

Now that you have been informed on what forex is and why it is a good idea to trade it, now it is time to learn how to open an account and how to trade currencies. There will also be some tips on how to be a success. This chapter is important to read carefully, as it will give you the basics of starting a forex trade.

Before you jump right into forex, though, there are several free sites that allow you to practice making an account and trading from there. A quick search online will show you just how easy it is to set up. This will give you a great practice and give you a leg up, as you decide to step into the real trading. As you practice, you will learn more about the market, and you will be able to navigate the real market rather easily.

These practice accounts are a good bench mark for how well you are n the market. If you can navigate them pretty easily, then you can be pretty sure that you will know enough to begin the process, but you should still proceed with a caution. These are just practices, and a lot can happen in the real market.

How to Set Up a Practice Account

https://www.fxcm.com/forex-trading-demo/ has the best practice accounts out there. So I will walk you through using this website. I have found it is the securest site, and you can also use it to set up a real account. The ease of which you can navigate it is also a plus. So we will start using this site.

1. Open your preferred web browser. I have found that it runs best on either Chrome of Mozilla Firefox. Internet Explorer is a little to buggy for this process. If you are on a Mac, Safari works just fine.

2. Input the web address https://www.fxcm.com/forex-trading-demo/ Make sure that you get it perfect, or you will be sent to a spammy ad site.

3. You will be prompted to input your name. If you don't feel comfortable with using your real name and want to use a pseudonym, it is important that you make one that is easy for you to remember, but it also has to be hard for someone else to guess. You also have to input your email, and phone number. I have made a new email that way I can find the emails easily. I also set up a new phone number on a free WI-FI text app. This way I know exactly which texts or calls are important.

4. Before you proceed to trading practice, you have to answer what level of trading experience you have. Answer that and you can proceed to the next page.

5. On this page, you will find your username and password. You should save these in a safe place. They will also be emailed to you, so save that email.

6. After you have saved your username and password, you can press start trading. This will open a new tab. This tab contains a log in screen.

7. Input your username and password into the login screen. Make sure that demo is selected in the section labeled connection.

8. You have the option to save login. I chose that as I am using a personal computer. If you are on a public computer, do not choose this.

9. Once you log in you will be able to start buying and selling investments.

10. It is simply laid out with tabs to find everything you need. Happy practicing.

This practice is very important so that you can get a feel for how the market works. There is a user guide under help, so if you have any issues, you can consult that and it explains everything you need to know in simple terms.

Tips to Making Yourself a Success

There are a few things that you must remember to be a success. This section will outline those for you in a simple way what those steps are, and things that you need to know. After reading this section you should have a better understanding of forex, and be able to feel confident in being able to open a practice account, and begin practicing on trading.

Forex is all about knowing when to sell, when to buy, and when to short sell. This is the hardest part. It is an educated waiting game. You cannot buy an exchange and then sell it in five minutes, You will lose a lot of profit. However, you also have to know when to sell. Sometimes it is better to sell sooner, rather than later, because if the market fluctuates too much, then it may crash in the exchange bracket you are in.

Things can change easily in this market, though you usually get a warning if they are going to change too drastically. You have to pay attention to the market somewhat, though it is not as strict as most markets in investing. So once you are into the investing, checking your account regularly is important. At least once a day. That way you are not staring at it tempted to sell at the first sign of increase, and you are not missing out on prime sell time.

Once you have established a time frame everyday to check your account, it is always best to make sure that you have a few days a week where you can watch it a little more. You need to be able to focus on it sometimes more than others, so you can get a feel for the market. More so in the beginning. You need to know exactly how the market works before you make a risky investment.

Here are some important things to remember when you are investing. Follow these things and you should find forex fairly easy.

Pairs

Every currency trade happens in pairs. You are concurrently buying and selling when you make a trade. For example if you are buying Euro, you are selling a US dollar, and vice-versa. This is an important thing to remember, because you have to receive more than you give. That is how you make a profit. So say you sell one US dollar in exchange for Yen. You would get 80.76 in Yen. This is how you make a good profit in this game. Learn the different exchange rates to proficiently navigate this market. Once you learn the different rates to every exchange, you will be able to make the most informed decision on what you should trade.

Commission

There are commission contracts that you have to take into account, and these can eat up your profit. You have to take into consideration all of the commissions you have to pay, and other fees. This lessens if you handle everything yourself, but in the beginning it is best not to try to go it alone.

Change

Things have changed in the last year. They are a little less risky due to more restrictions on trades. This means you will have to put in a little more money at times, but this is for the best, because there is less risk for major loss. However it is important to keep this in mind so you don't get discouraged when you aren't making as much as your friend in the business did last year. The National Futures Association restricted trade ratios on well known trades from one hundred to one down to fifty to one. Obscure trades were reduced from their current ratio down to twenty five to one. This reduces risk by a great amount, which makes forex a more enjoyable platform.

Size

This began as an investment opportunity for big firms. Keeping that in mind, you have to realize that these firms can invest a lot more money than the average person. That means that they will be able to make a bigger profit than the average Joe. They also have a bigger threshold for loss. You as a single investor, do not. This means that you probably should only invest a portion into forex. Put your other money in savings to hedge any loss you may have. If you succeed, you still should have some caution with further investments. Investment markets of any kind can be volatile.

Use Caution

You should never put your trust in anything that promises a big return in a few short hours or days. You have to use your logical part of your brain rather than the emotional side. There should always be a warning bell that sounds off in your head when you see something that is too good to be true. Because in the world of investing, of any kind of investing, if it is to good to be true, it generally is.

The thing about investing is there is a lot of scams floating around. You have to be careful. Unfortunately, as humans, we are programmed to follow our emotions more than our cognitive thinking skills. You have to follow your logic in this industry, which means that you have to retrain your mind. That can be difficult. The best way to achieve this is meditation. You have to learn to calm yourself. Once you can control your reactions properly, you will be great in the market.

The best investors are able to keep a level head even in the face of the strongest persuasion.

If you can think logically rather than emotionally you will be okay.

Weakness/vs Strength

You have to know what you are good at and what you are not. You have to have a basic grip of these things so you know what you need to work on to become better in the market. Really pay attention to how you operate in this system. Do you sell too soon? Do you wait too long? Are you too easily excited? Not excitable enough? Once you know what your weaknesses are, you can figure out what you need to work on in order to become a success.

If you know your strengths, that is great as well, you can always hone those as well, but do not forget to give your weaknesses some attention as well. That is why you should always take care to make yourself the best you can be.

Revenge is NOT the Answer

You have to be very careful not to try to get revenge on the market after a bad investment. You will most certainly fail. Failure is not a good thing. You have to be level headed. This goes along with not thinking with your emotions. You have to separate yourself from the market. If you are not level headed and you try to get revenge on the market, then you will end up making to many risky investments, and that is a big mistake, as you cannot expect to come out on top when you have more than one risky investment in play. If you have a level head, then you can easily succeed a lot better than if you are enraged by a failure. Just take it as a mistake, and then walk away.

Planning

Unlike most investment markets, you have to develop your own plan, rather than using someone else's. This market is very customized, and specific because you are only working on your time. This is very important to remember.

But you must first make yourself a plan. You can't expect to make any money if you are flailing around blindly in the dark. Any type of investment requires a lot of planning, and figuring things out. You have to sit down, and plan out exactly what your goals are, and how you are going to approach each investment into forex. You cannot go into it and just click a few buttons and expect to make a huge profit. You may get lucky a couple times, but you won't survive that way for long. To get consistent results, you must have a plan every time.

Research

On top of planning, you have to do your research. While this is a pretty easy sector of investing to understand, you still have to learn about the workings of the business. You have to know where to start, and how to do so. This book is a good starter for that research, but there are several others out there that are good as well. The more informed you are about this business, the more success you have a chance of gaining. Research is a good thing, and spending just a few hours learning will leave you with a lifetime of success.

Mindset

You have to have the right mindset, and you have to avoid the thought that you cannot do this and many other thoughts as well. This is how many people lose in this business. They go in too skeptical, and don't believe that they will really make it. They think that it takes too much time or that it is too difficult. You have to go in with the mindset that you are going to succeed. You have to be confident, or else you will get nowhere.

This does not mean be cocky. That is the other end of the failure spectrum. You have to be humble, but confident. A little bit of a paradox if you will. Know that you will succeed, but be aware that it will take some hard work. You aren't just going to have money fall on your feet. It is more confidence in yourself that you need, rather than confidence in the market. Be confident that you have what it takes to make it big.

Brokers

This is important. If you do not want to get lost the first few investments you make, it is important to imbibe the help of a broker to handle your first few transactions. They will walk you through the process, and answer any questions you may have about the business, and help you understand everything you need to know.

The kicker in this is that you have to make sure that the broker is reputable. Some people will claim that they can be your broker and either lose all your money or rip you off. If you do not check credentials, you can be in for a world of hurt as you are just starting out. Always ask questions, read reviews, and make sure they are certified. If they refuse to show you certificates, or there are no reviews on them, keep walking. You should only want to trust the best with your future.

Diversity

The best way to minimize loss is to add diversity. This does not mean a lot of different risky investments, but a lot of different trades. The more diverse you are, then you can make sure that even if one market area crashes, you will be covered in another area. Say the value of the Yen plummets, and you only have orders dealing in Yen. You will be in for a big shock as you see that you have lost all of your profit. As this happens though, maybe the value of the Australian Dollar skyrocketed. If you also had some orders in Australian dollars, you would be able to cover the loss of the Yen with the Australian dollar.

The thing about diversity is, the more diverse you are, the less risk you can take, because your resources are spread out across the board, that is where the risk lies. You are going to be out of your comfort zone some of the time. That is okay, because even though you feel like this is where the risk is, it is actually the safest route to go, as long as you go with relatively safe orders.

Know yourself

This goes with knowing your strengths and your weaknesses. You have to know your risk threshold, and how far you can push yourself before you start making mistakes. If you do not know this,you will continuously push yourself too far, or stop too short. You have to know what you are capable of, and subsequently, what you are not.

This means you have to pay attention to how you operate in the practice accounts. Write down your processes to success, and what you did to cause a failure. By studying yourself, you can figure out where your risk threshold is, and you will be able to take that with you when you open a real account. Once you open a real account, it is best to stay a bit below your risk threshold in the beginning, because otherwise you will be in for a big shock because it is a little different in the real world.

Account types

There are different accounts that you can open. You need to know what they are so that you can make the best decision for you. There are three major account types.

- **Managed Account**: This has the highest minimum deposit required, and it depends on the broker that handles it. You have to have around ten thousand dollars, but this is the least stressful, because the broker assigns a professional trader to your account to make the money for you. However, that is more people that you have to pay with your profit. There are pros and cons for this one, and it is definitely an account for the better off financially.

- **Standard Account**: This is the medium account. Most brokers have set the minimum deposit at two thousand dollars, though for some it can be higher, and some it can be lower. This account has a decent amount of leverage, and a guarantee for limited risk. The minimum lot size is ten thousand dollars, so that is some decent leverage.

- **Mini Account:** Just as the name states, this account is the smallest account you can get. Like the others, the minimum deposit is set by separate brokers, but the average is two hundred dollars. While it has the guarantee on limited risk like the Standard Account, it has less leverage, and a way higher spread, meaning your bids are more risky, and the outcome is not as great. With two hundred you will be lucky to control a two thousand five hundred dollar account.

Those are the types of accounts that you will find through most brokers. They may be under different names, but the concept will be the same. Once you decide how much money you have to invest, you can then decide on the type of account you need for your investment. You have to choose the right type of account or you will get in over your head, and that is not a good thing.

Losing Positions

This should go without saying, but don't add to a losing position. However, most people are certain that there will be a turnaround in their position as this market is notorious for that, but with new regulations, it is not as common as it used to be for turnarounds to happen soon enough to save you from losing a lot of money. Most people are still in the trading mindset of years prior, because the new regulations are not very well known, and it is hard to break old habits. Thankfully for you, you are coming into the market with fresh views, so you will know about these regulations and be able to adapt to them a lot easier than someone who has been in this for years.

Automate

In today's forex trading, it is so easy to automate everything, however you must automate everything yourself. This does not mean use a machine to do your trading for you. You have to automate yourself to make this work. Rather than taking even a logical approach to trading, take a methodical approach. Follow tried and true patterns from the market. Make your decisions almost like an algorithm. If you can do that, you will have the best success, because you will be able to make a perfect decision nearly every time.

However, do not use actual automation, such as forex robots. These are just scams to make money for their sellers. Forex robots are computer bots that you instal, and they are supposed to monitor your account, and make deals for you, but their commission rates are high, and they often come with a lot of viruses. It is best to stay away from these if you wish to actually make a profit. You might make a profit a couple of times, but it will be just like making an emotional trade, a sheet of pure luck. You can't let an automated robot make your decisions for you. You have to make your own.

Simplicity

You have to keep your trading simple, otherwise when it gets complicated, you will get confused. Simplicity allows you to approach each trade easily without worry of remembering complicated steps in a really long process. The simpler things are, the better you have at succeeding.

Markets

Do not fight the market. You are just one grain of sand on a giant beach. Stay humble, and remember that if you allow the market to carry you, you will get a lot farther than you would if you try to fight it. Work on accommodating your failures, because most of the time they cannot be eliminated completely. You have to work with them, not try to rid of them entirely. It will take less effort to incorporate them into your trade rather than try to sell them for the best outcome possible. Who knows, they might even turn into success then.

Money Management

Once most people start making a profit, they start to get a little reckless with it. You have to be able to manage your money. There are many different resources that you can get access to that will teach you how to manage your money. Make use of these resources so that you can optimize your profit to the fullest extent. You have to be able to make the best use of your money otherwise you may end up losing any profit you make by getting to excited about having profit, that you might over spend.

Start Small

Of course with investing, you think, big sums, big profit, so you are inclined to make a big trade. However, that is not the way to go when you don't quite understand the market like a pro. Start small, and see how you do that way to minimize risk. When you start small, you have less money to lose that way, and you can judge your risk threshold better that way. Once you understand the market, you can start to trade with larger sums.

Understanding

Only do what you understand. If you don't understand a trade, it is best to shy away from it. This is just common sense, but a lot of people don't see it that way. You have to stay within the bounds of what you know. If you want to do something a little trickier, study it, and take it to a practice account first before you branch out. This way, you can learn it, and you won't fall flat on your face like you would if you jumped in without understanding the process.

Stay Strong

You are going to have failures. That is something that is unavoidable. Nobody can succeed the first time they try something. No matter how much you think you know the investment market, forex is a whole new world. It is unlike any other type of investing out there, and because it is so unique, you have to learn a whole new set of rules. So if you don't make a profit your first try, that is okay. Just keep trying. After a few tries, you should start making a profit, and then you can continue from there.

Don't get discouraged if you don't do as well as you did in the practice accounts either. It is a different world in the real accounts. The practice accounts are just to help you understand how to buy and sell your orders. They are merely there to help you understand the process better. They are not a benchmark for how you will do in the real market, just a guide to navigating the accounts.

Learn from your failures as well. Rather than getting discouraged, let your failures motivate you, because even Albert Einstein said "I did not fail, I merely found a thousand ways to do it wrong." Use this mindset to keep you going. Every mistake is one step closer to finding the way that works for you. You have to fall before you can fly, and you have to stumble before you can walk.

Focus On One Area

Focus on a single currency pair that you can understand in the beginning. Once you have a grip on that pair, you can move onto another pair that you understand fairly well. As you learn about more pairs, you can move onto the next pairs. Once you learn about those pairs, you can add even more into your repertoire.

If you try to start with trading too many currency pairs in the beginning, you will get overwhelmed, and you will not be able to focus on making a profit, because you will be too busy trying to keep from losing too much money in your many different currency pairs. So while it is good to have diversity, let the diversity come with time.

Timing

You have to time your entries just right. Find a time where the market is at a stable place, and make your bid. Once you have established a good foundation, then you can go from there. You also have to time your sales just right. If you don't sell at the right time, you could miss on on good profit, or even lose money. Be patient and let the money make itself after you make the bid.

Adapt

This market fluctuates, and there are changes. The best traders are flexible, and can adapt easily. You have to be willing and able to adapt to anything this market throws at you, otherwise you will break. Being stiff on your trades can cause you a lot of headache, as you favorite market may crash, and if you are hanging on too tight, it will drag you down with it.

If you are a type A personality, you are going to have to retrain yourself to step outside of your comfort zone, and become adaptable. You cannot always just stick with what you know. You have to be able to go with what makes you a little uncomfortable as well. You still have to be knowledgeable about the area you are stepping into, but you can't focus only on one area. You have to be able to make changes to your plan as well.

No Stop Hunting

Most brokers look for stops that will give you a profit, but minimize your time on the market. This can cause a problem because they are potentially limiting your ability to make a profit as well. You have to put a stop to this. Make sure that you inform your broker that you do not want any stops hunting on your account. Let them know that you will not accept any type of that behavior. Get it in writing so you can ensure that you are protected from them doing that.

Expectations

Just like with any type of investing, this is a business, not a lottery. You cannot expect to make a million dollars in a week. This business takes time and effort to get anywhere in. You have to be willing to put in that time and effort if you want to succeed. A lot of people expect to make a lot of money in a short amount of time, and that is just not the case here. You have to have reasonable expectations when you are going into this. Otherwise you will get discouraged. You have to be reasonable with what you expect from this market.

Expecting too much from yourself can be a problem as well. As stated in ab above tip, you can't expect to get it all right the first try. You are going to fail a few times, and it will seem like you will never get it right. If you keep trying though, you eventually will get it right, but if you keep your expectations too high, you will give up before you succeed. Keep them low, so that any success will be a pleasant surprise, but also don't keep them so low that you expect to fail every time. It is a fine line to walk between too high expectations and having expectations that are too low.

Be Reasonable

Along with your expectations, you need to be reasonable with your trade amount. You should not be anywhere near draining your account with any trade. You should only have a portion of your account on any one trade. One tenth is almost too much. You do not want to risk losing too much money, so always try to be reasonable on a trade.

You also have to be reasonable with the amount of time you hold your trade. Some people hold their trades for too short of a time, and some people hold them for too long. You have to find a happy medium, and hold your trade for that amount of time to get the optimum profit you can receive from that trade. Holding on for too long can leave you at risk for a market crash, and not holding it for long enough can leave you at risk for not making a lot of profit.

Patience

This has been the theme for all of the tips it seems. You have to have patience to succeed, because otherwise you will sell too soon, or you will get discouraged because you are not making enough money. It can take up to nine months to get a good amount of profit on one single trade. While others can take five minutes. You cannot use the time benchmark for one trade for all of your trades. You have to use profit margin as your benchmark. Even then that can get tricky. But this game is of patience. Much like a manta ray sits on the ocean and waits for its prey, you must sit on the web and wait for your trade to make its profit.

The best way to be patient is to not stare at your account. Check it periodically, and then log back off. Do what you need to when logged on, but if your profit is still building, then let it build. However you have to have a good balance of patience and interest. You have to stay vigilant so you can sell at the best time, but you can't sell too early.

Discipline

You have to have self discipline to keep yourself from going over the deep end and losing a lot of money. Self discipline helps you retrain your mind from the mindset that you can lead with your emotions and you will be fine. You have to input some self discipline, and allow yourself to automate everything through your own processes. Most forex traders that fail, did not exercise any self discipline.

Discipline also applies to sticking to a plan, and not straying from it because you see a shiny new trade opportunity. You have to stick to your guns, and not be distracted by promises of fortune in a few short days. Make sure to stay on top of your learning curve. Even if you feel you know enough, never settle for basic learning, always yearn to learn more. Discipline your mind. You will be a bigger success than you ever dreamed.

No Averaging

I put that in all caps to be sure I have your attention. This is not an average market. You simply cannot average your losses, and expect to make any money. You have to follow the curve at that moment. Otherwise you will be struck with a huge loss. Exclude averaging from your mind. Forget about the word entirely. Just forget it. Zip. Gone.

Journal

Keep a journal. This is important to do. You can track your every success, and every failure, and you will start to see a pattern that you can use to lessen your failures, and exceed your current successes. A journal will also help you keep in line with your plan, and you can go back and refer to it whenever you hit a tricky situation.

Even if you do not hit a tricky situation, you should still consult your journal every couple of weeks or so. This will be good for motivation, as you see how far you have come since you started, and you will also be able to see what you need to adjust to make yourself go even farther.

Keep Your Demo

Just because you have hit the real account level does not mean you have to get rid of your demo account. There are many purposes it could serve even after you hit the account level. You can go back to practice around when you are getting discouraged. This will help you get motivated again as you can see what you are capable of when you take some pressure off yourself to succeed.

You can also use your demo account when you are wanting to try new things. This will allow you to have a risk free environment to try out these new things, and learn more about them, so that you do not mess up when you have real money on the line. You can also use it to get a refresher on what you already know if you have been away from it for a while.

It is also fun to just go back and see what you can do with a demo account, to give yourself a confidence boost, and get back to enjoying trading again. Just like with any other business you are in, once the spark is gone, you will start to fail more and more because you just wont care. You have to bring that spark back into your trades. A demo account can help with this, because there is no pressure to succeed, and you can do some silly things and have fun again.

Those are some tips for you to succeed, and how to navigate a forex account. Follow these and you will succeed without question. Always remember that forex is a tricky market at times, and though it is easy to learn, sometimes it is not as easy to navigate. You just have to be flexible, and ready to make a profit.

Chapter 4: How to Make this a Part Time Job

Forex may seem like it is not substantial enough to become a part time job, but that is the farthest from the truth. There are many ways that you can make it a part time job, and make enough profit to consider it an income. You just have to be prepared to put in some effort, rather than just sit back and let the money make itself.

There are a few things you have to consider about making this a profession, rather than a hobby that makes you a little extra money.

Time

Do you have enough time to focus on this, because when you are actively trying to use this as a source of income, you have to focus more on it than you would if you are just trying it out as a hobby.

Effort

Are you willing to put the effort needed into this? Making a substantial profit from this business is possible, but it takes effort, and research. You have to be willing to put your best foot forward.

Focus

Are you able to focus a certain amount of time each day on this business? If you have kids, can you get some time away from them long enough to get some work done?

Knowledge

Do you have any knowledge about what it takes to actually make this a profession? If not, are you willing to learn? You have to be knowledgeable about forex to make it a profession. You can't just breeze your way through it as if it were just a game you want to play.

Expectations

How high are your expectations? Are they reasonable? You have to have reasonable expectations for this business. You can't just jump right into something and expect to be great at it. Same with making it better. It takes time.

Flexibility

Are you flexible enough for this market? You have to be flexible, and willing to adapt to this market. If you aren't this cannot be a part time profession, because the more time you spend with it, the more adaptation it requires.

If you can handle all of these things, then you would be great as a part time forex trader. This is a great thing, because you can make a great supplemental income from it, without having to work in a hot building all day, greeting people, and you can just sit back in your pajamas and watch your orders for changes.

Chapter 5: Attitude for Winning

Your attitude is a big part of your success. You have to have the right mindset otherwise you will not be as big of a success as you would be if you are in the right mindset. This business is all about the right thoughts.

Here are a few things that you should think, and what you should avoid thinking.

Good Thoughts

- **Confident**

  Having confident thoughts is essential to being a success. Visualize your success, and you will achieve it. You have to see yourself as a successful person, and you have to think that you will make it. This is ninety percent of what you need to think to be good at this industry.

- **Future**

  You have to visualize where you want to be at in the future. Set a goal, and pursue it the best you can. Once you have the visualized target, keep it in mind, for you to reach towards. You have to have something to work towards otherwise you will be too easily discouraged.

- **Possibility**

  You have to have the mindset that this industry is possible, otherwise you will not make it very far. You have to stay positive, even if you are having a few struggles along the way. It is not perfect, but it is possible, if you just believe in yourself.

- **Market**

  You have to think about the market, and realize that it is very slippery. You have to be in the mindset of a pig wrangler almost. If you keep one step ahead of the pig, eventually you will catch it. Even though it changes directions fast, you will have the mindset of the market, so you will be anticipating the changes.

- **Motivation**

  You have to motivate yourself constantly. This market can be very discouraging, and that is not the easiest thing to work through. Just take some time out when you get discouraged, and go back and see how far you have come to motivate yourself again.

Bad Thoughts

- **Can't**

  This word should never cross your thoughts. The minute you think you can't is the minute you decide to fail. You have to think that you can make this trade, and you have to believe you will succeed.

- **Time**

  This is the biggest fail precedent You think that something will take too much time, so you pass it up for the quicker option. This is a big mistake, because just because something takes a little longer does not mean it is not worth it.

Chapter 6: Recap

There was a lot of information in this book, and I hope you thoroughly enjoyed reading it, as well as got the information you needed. Let's have a rundown of all of the important things that were covered in this book.

What Forex Is

Forex is the trading of foreign currencies to make a profit. It is a type of investment that is simple enough that someone who has never heard of investing can learn in a few weeks the basics of this business. Forex has been around as long as people had currency, which is pretty much since the beginning of time.

Why You Should Trade Forex

It is a great way to make a supplemental income, and it does not take a whole lot of time to do. You have the option of flexible hours as well, so it can fit into your schedule whenever you want it to. Also, it does not take a constant watchful eye, so you can go about your business without worry.

How to Succeed

You have to do your research on this business to succeed. That is what most of it breaks down to. If you do your research you will be able to handle the market with ease, because you will be able to handle anything it throws at you.

How to Make it a Profession

This can become a part time profession if you allow it to be. You just have to allot some time to focus on it, and make sure that you are able to be adaptable. This is not the easiest to make a profession, but once you do, the money will be worth it.

Attitude to Succeed

You have to have a positive mindset. You have to truly believe you can do it, and be confident. Don't over think things too much, or else you will ruin your chances of success.

That is the information of each chapter all broken down into a few short sentences. Of course you can't use this recap to fuel your success, but it is a good thing to look back on to reference what you need.

Conclusion

I hope you enjoyed reading this book on forex, and I hope that you found it educational, and interesting. This book was designed to motivate you, and give you the info you need to feel comfortable in opening your own account, and start forex trading. Thank you again for downloading this e-book.

If you enjoyed it, please feel free to leave a review on Amazon.

Happy exchanging!

www.ingramcontent.com/pod-product-compliance
Lightning Source LLC
Chambersburg PA
CBHW061202180526
45170CB00002B/918